Coloring Book

Cool Vehicles

This Book

belongs to.............

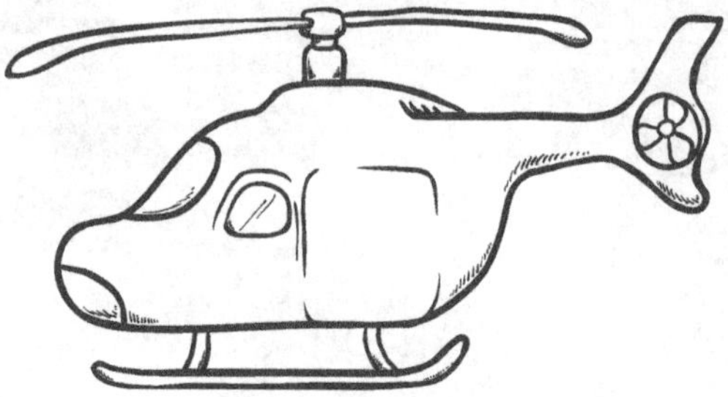

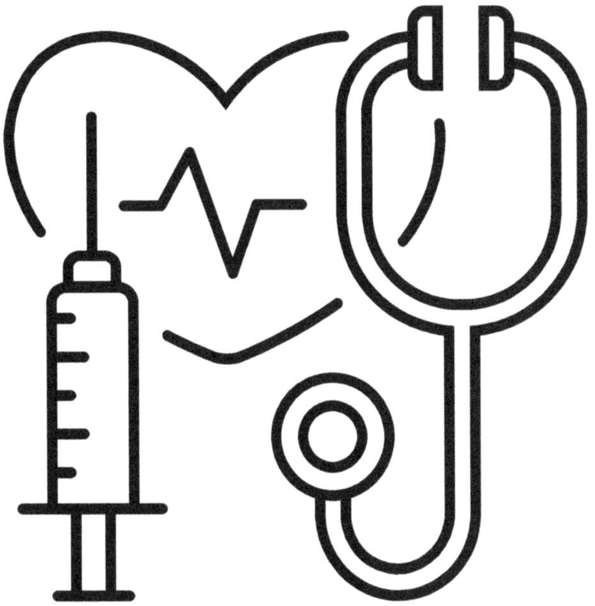

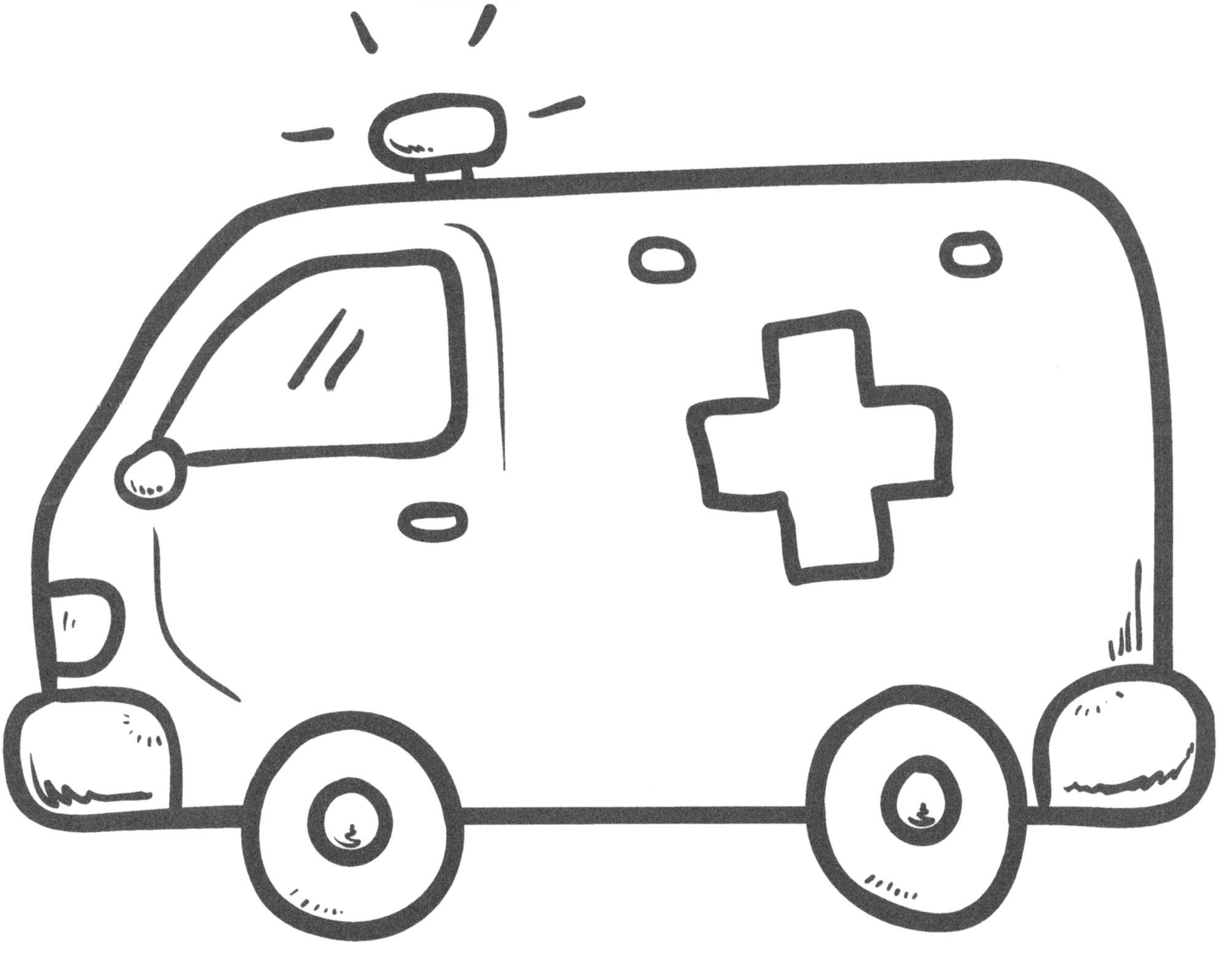

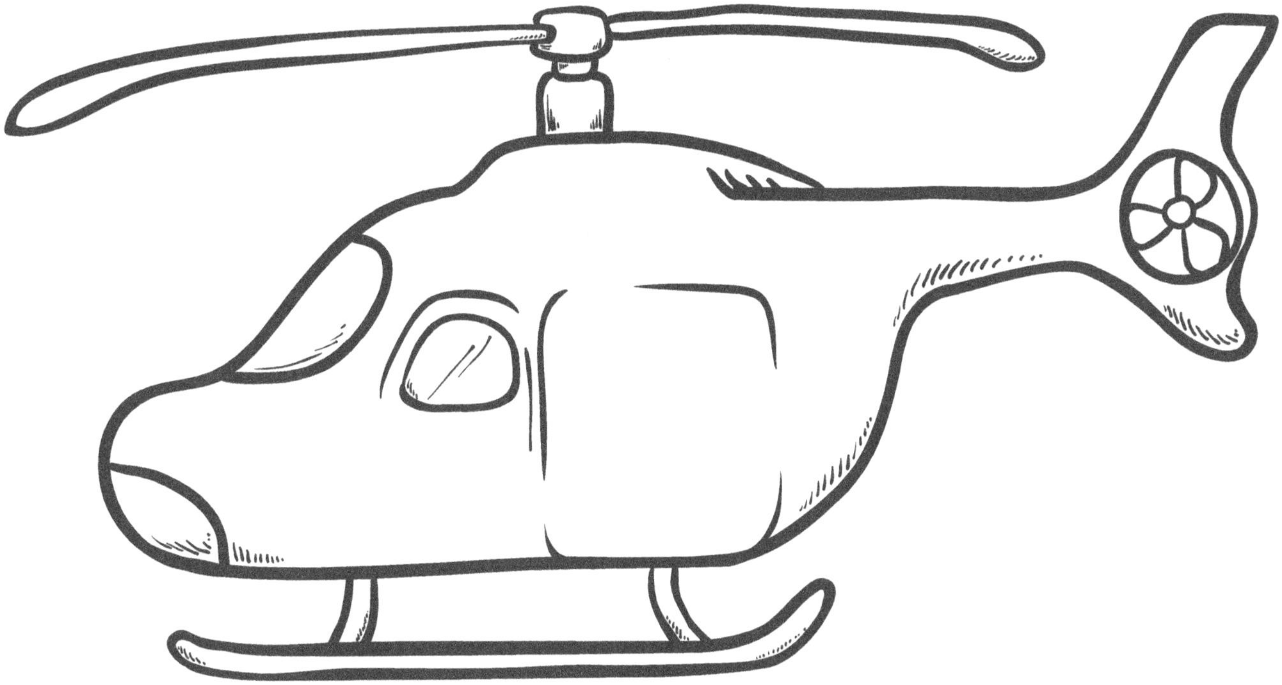

MAIL

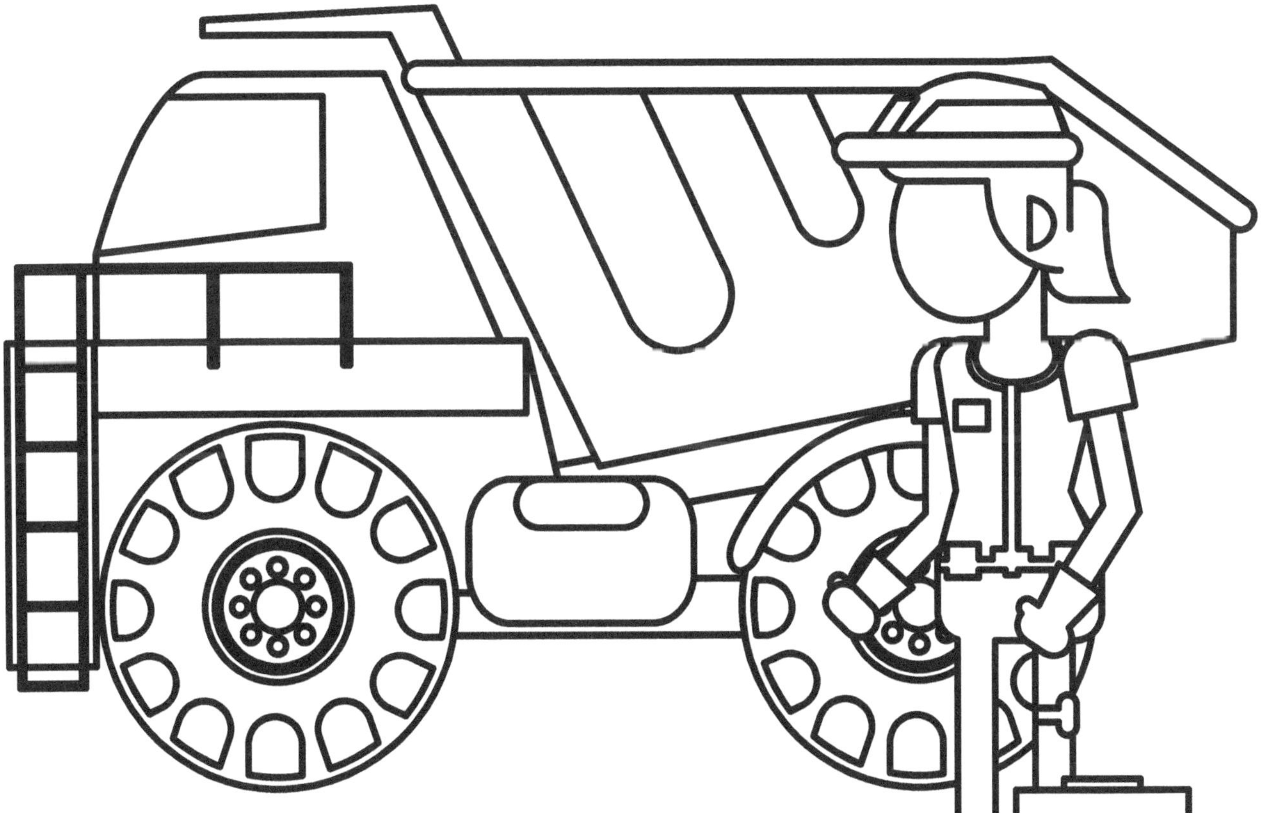

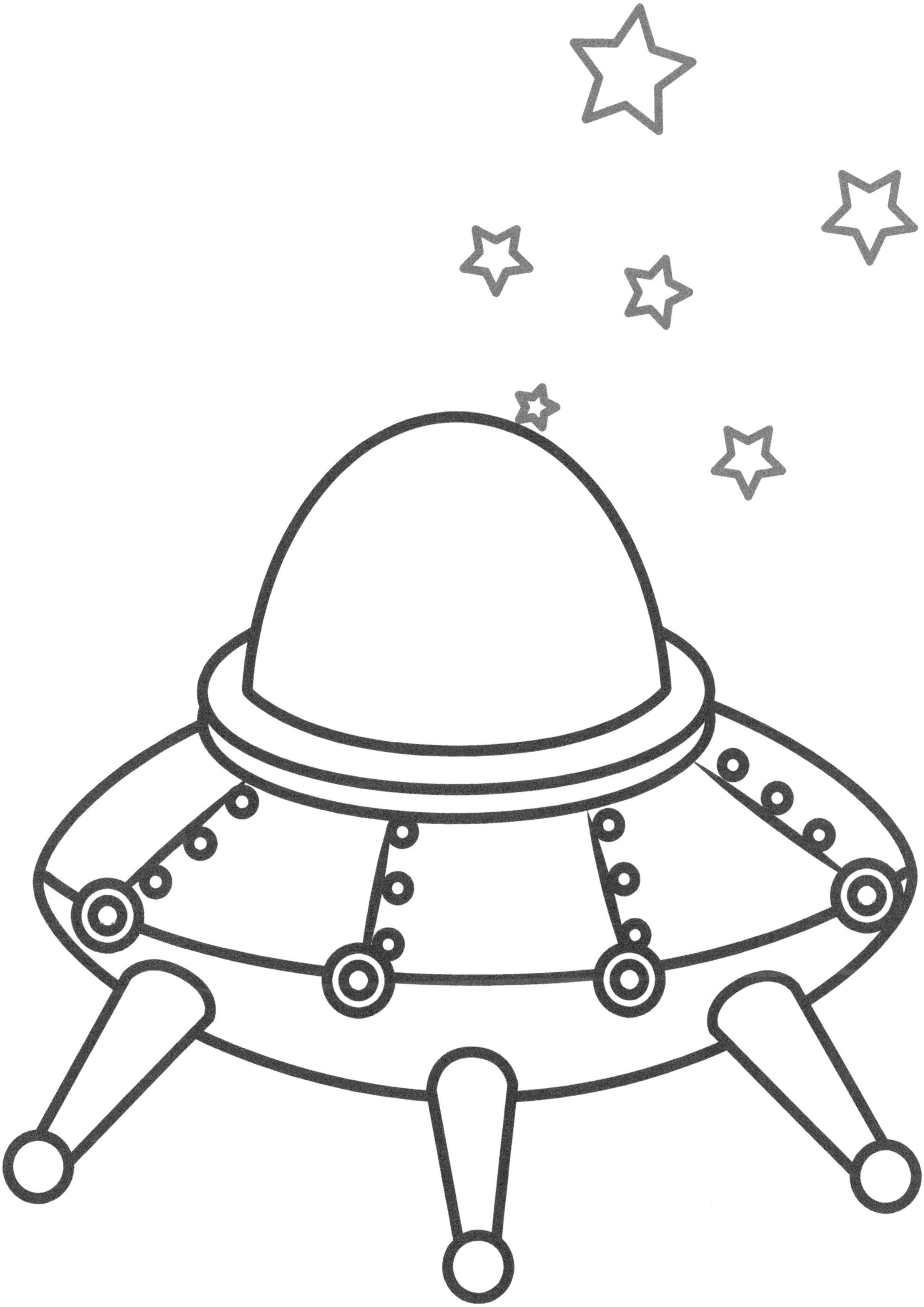

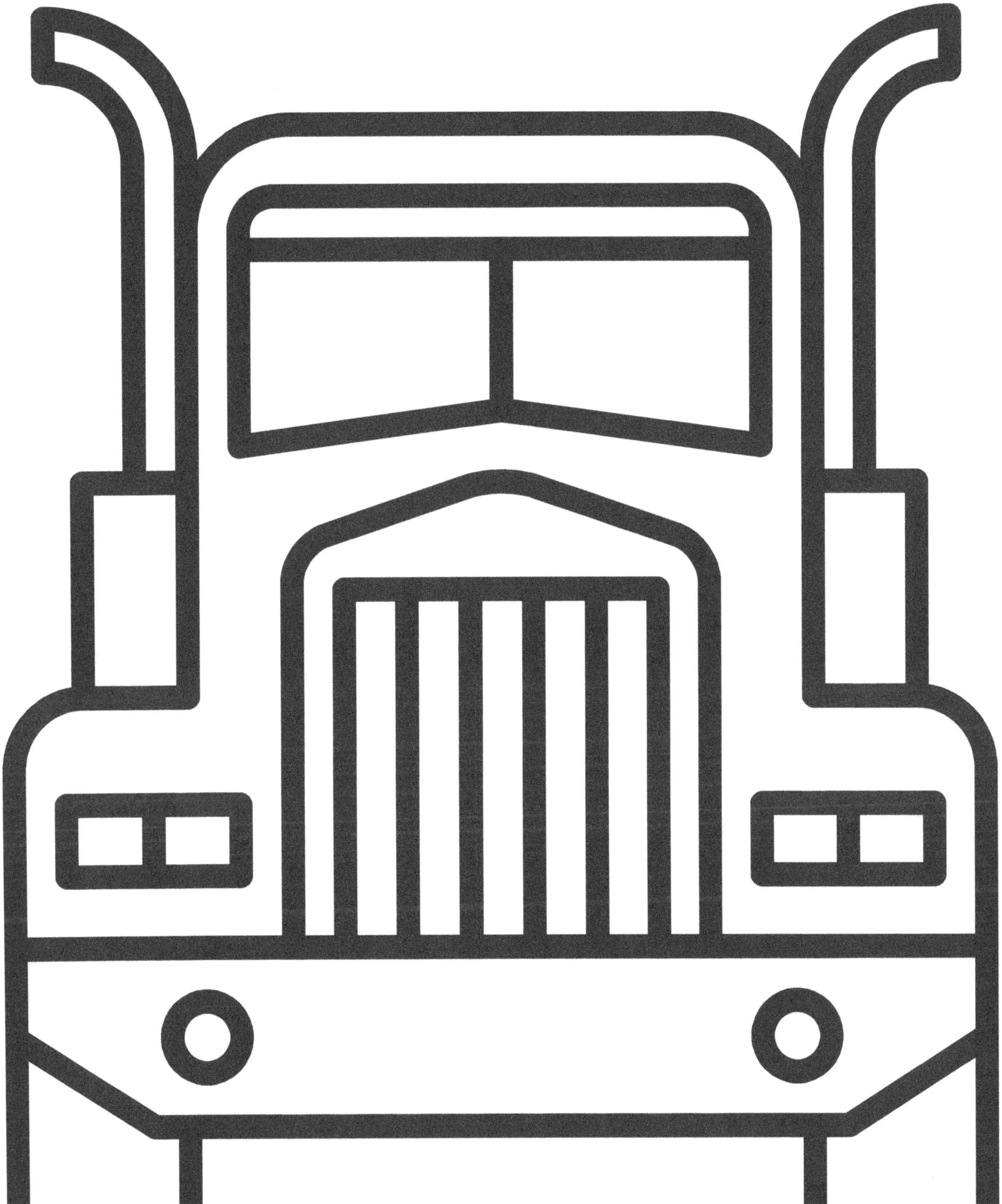

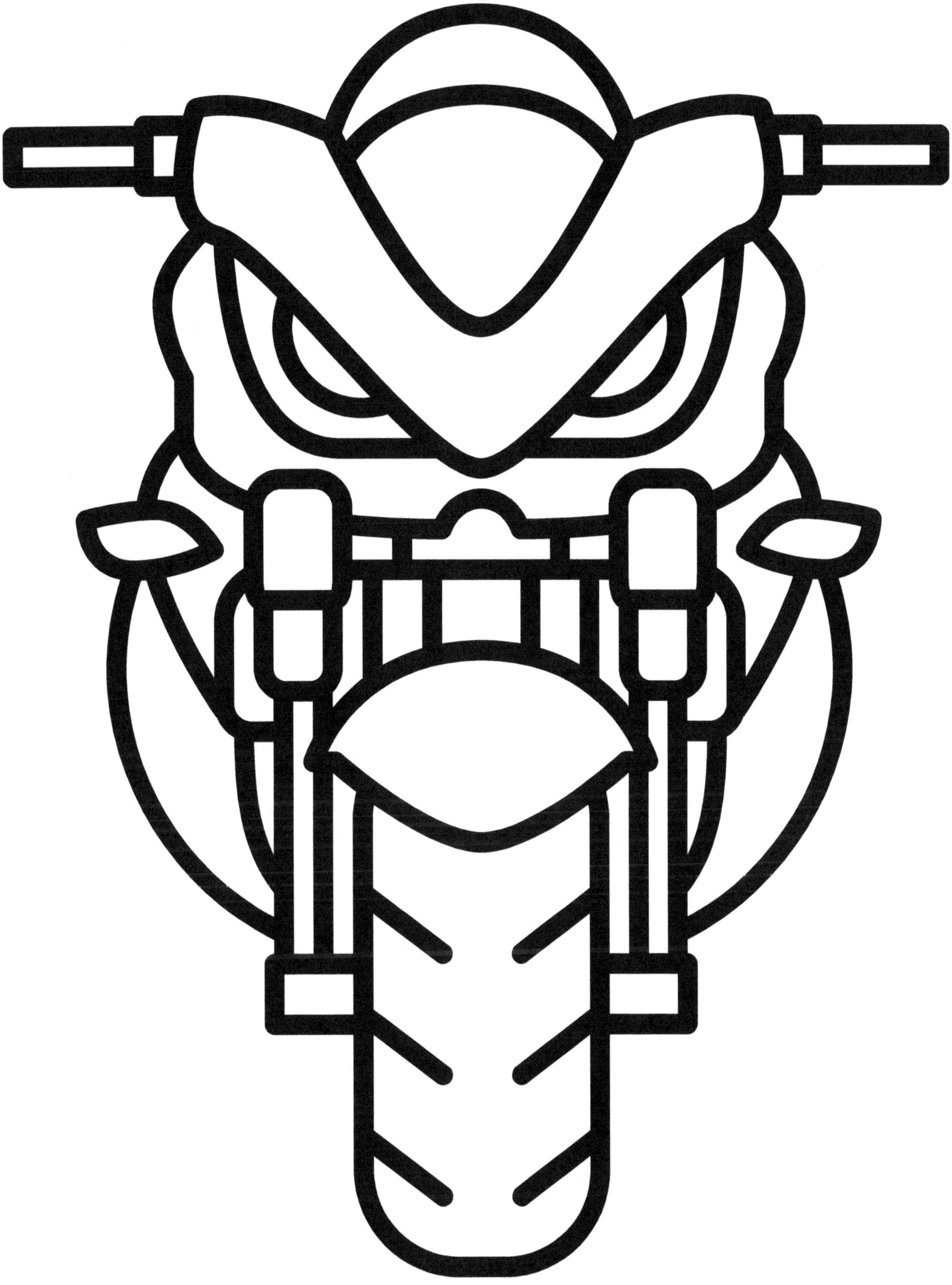

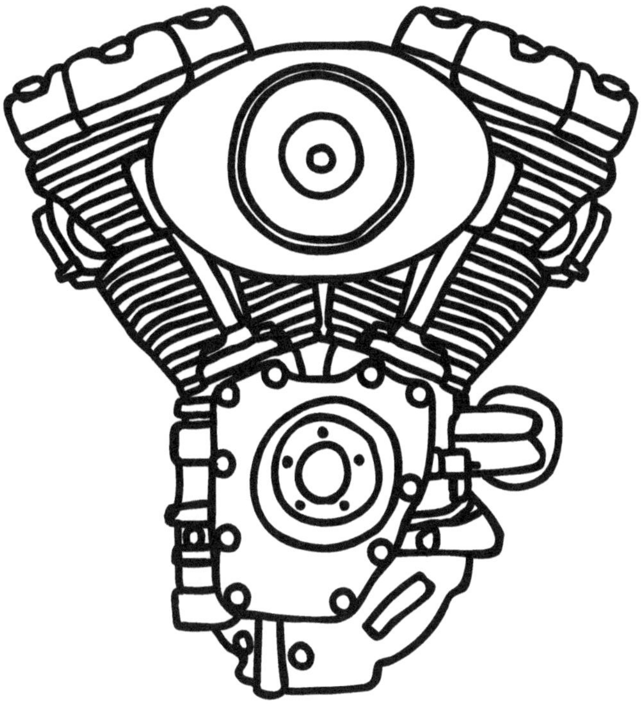

POLICE

CPSIA information can be obtained
at www.ICGtesting.com
Printed in the USA
BVHW011557130521
607263BV00003B/187

9 783551 118998